The Bible

The Absolute Authority For
Faith And Practice

By Pastor Robert Dickie

ISBN: 978-1-7346822-5-0

Table of Contents

Martin Luther with his Bible

Introduction

The culture that our children are growing up in is a culture of relativity. It is a culture that believes there are no absolutes. It is also a culture that does not recognize the Bible to be any kind of authority over us, let alone to be the Word of the living God. Young people today are no different from any of those in the past. Everyone, both young or old, wants to know what is right and wrong and why these things are right and wrong. Youth is especially a time for asking questions such as these. However, because of the societal attacks on the authority and integrity of the Word of God, most young people are not willing to accept the Bible as the basis for their moral beliefs. This is precisely why we have so many problems today. This current culture has undermined, ridiculed, and attacked the Bible, which has destroyed the very foundation for ethics and morality. After destroying this generation's faith in the Bible, we are left wondering why this same generation is wandering in a maze of confusion and moral depravity. It should not be a mystery as to why so many people today commit such horrific crimes involving mass shootings, murder, rape, theft, and display unkindness to other people. If we ask today's young people any question about ethics or morality, they are without any real authority to support their answers. Only the Bible can provide an authoritative basis for our beliefs and convictions. Only by the authority of the Bible can we answer the following questions:

- Why is lying wrong?
- Why is stealing wrong?
- Why is murder wrong?
- Why is slavery wrong?
- Why is euthanasia wrong?
- Why is abortion wrong?
- Why is adultery wrong?
- Why is unkindness wrong?
- Why is rebellion wrong?
- Why is disobedience to parents wrong?
- Why is taking God's name in vain wrong?
- Why is coveting what other people have wrong?
- Why is it wrong to be rude to people?
- Why is it wrong to destroy public property?
- Why is it wrong to threaten and bully people?
- Why is it wrong to throw bricks through windows and loot stores?

- Why is it wrong to use bigoted and rude speech to other people?

Whatever answers young people may give to these questions, if they reject the Bible as the absolute authority for all moral issues of right and wrong, then they have no moral authority to support any of their answers. We may ask them, "By what authority do you say that?" "How do you know that is true?" "How do you know that you are right?" "What makes your answer right and someone else's answer wrong?" "Your answer is arbitrary." Without the absolute authority of God's holy law, anyone's opinion is as good as another's.

Not only does the Bible give us the moral authority to make judgments on the great issues of life, the Bible also gives us the ability to recognize false convictions that are being presented as proper moral standards. For example, when young college students today claim that Christopher Columbus was a genocidal maniac, or that slavery was a terrible institution, or that all white people are racists, what gives them any moral authority to make such statements?

How can protesters and activists justify their hatred, violence, and vulgarity when insulting, attacking, and beating down all opposition? How can someone excuse this kind of behavior? A Harvard grad posted on social media that the next person she heard say, "All lives matter" she would stab with a knife, and as they were dying and bleeding out she would taunt them by holding up her finger with a paper cut and say, "My cut matters too!" How is it that this young woman had no moral compass to actually see how vile, hateful, bitter, and morally repugnant she is? This young woman, like millions of people, is ignorant of the teachings of God's law.

If the God of the Bible is denied, we cannot account for reason, logic, ethics, morality, and even our own existence. Without the God of the Bible nothing in the world will make any sense at all. Without the God of the Bible the possibility of evil is limitless. History has taught us that the Christian worldview has been the greatest deterrent to evil in the world and the most positive benefit to the spread of law, ethics, and morality. If the Bible is rejected the doors of evil are thrown wide open and the horrors that rush through her gates will know no limits. How do we prove the Bible to a young person? To prove that the Bible is the Word of God and that it is true in every area where it speaks, we need to first ask a few questions. These questions will be the outline that we will follow to pursue this objective of demonstrating the truthfulness of the Bible. The questions are:

- What Is The Bible?
- Why Is The Bible True?
- Why Is The Bible Important?

1
What Is The Bible?

The Bible is the Word of God. The Bible tells us that it is the Word of God. We would not know that the Bible is the Word of God if it did not make this claim. The Bible tells us that God breathed out His very words on the pages of Scripture and that His Holy Spirit moved the authors of the Scripture to pen the very words they wrote. One author clarified what was meant by the concept that the Bible was the Word of God. This author states:

"The Bible is the Word of God. Yes, various human authors wrote it—but behind them was another Author: the Spirit of God. Even when they weren't fully aware of it, God was guiding them so that what they wrote wasn't just their own words, but God's Word. The apostle Peter wrote, "No prophecy of Scripture came about by the prophet's own interpretation. For prophecy never had its origin in the will of man, but men spoke from God as they were carried along by the Holy Spirit" (2 Peter 1:20-21). God wanted to speak to us in words we could understand—and the Bible contains those words. The Bible isn't just a collection of men's ideas about God, nor is it a guidebook for living that people developed over the centuries. It is the Word of God—and that makes all the difference. This means the Bible is our authority in everything it touches. This means the Bible is our guide to show us how to live. Most of all, this means the Bible is our instructor, teaching us about God and His plan of salvation in Christ. The Old Testament points toward Christ's coming; the New Testament tells of His arrival. From Genesis to Revelation we see God's great plan unfold—His plan to win a lost humanity back to Himself. The central theme of the Bible is salvation, and the central personality of the Bible is Christ.

The Bible is God's gift to us. It came from God, and it points us to God. The Bible says of itself, "All Scripture is given by inspiration of God, and is profitable for doctrine, for reproof, for correction, for instruction in righteousness, that the man of God may be complete, thoroughly equipped for every good work" (2 Timothy 3:16-17 NKJV)."[1]

The Bible is a collection of 66 books written over a period of approximately 1500 years by 40 different authors. These books are divided into the Old and New Testaments. The Old Testament contains 39 books and the New Testament contains 27 books. Some of the amazing features of the Bible are that it contains no contradictions, has one great theme, (blood redemption through the finished work of Jesus Christ), and has been preserved over the years from errors of addition and subtraction through the process of copying it from age to age.

How was it determined which books should be included in the Bible? This is an important question. If any books that should be in the Bible were left out or disregarded, then it could be argued that the Bible is not complete and perhaps is missing key information that might alter how we view the Christian faith. The books that are contained in the Bible are referred to as the Biblical canon. The English word "canon" in the Greek means "rule" or "measuring stick." The Biblical canon is the collection of books that make up the Holy Scriptures. These books or sacred writings were inspired by God and given to His covenant people. The canon of Scripture had been decided upon at a very early date (by the time of Christ) for the Old Testament books. The Jewish historian, Josephus of the first century, listed 22 Old Testament books accepted by the Jews, which appear to match our current 39-book collection. The New Testament books were decided upon by the end of the second century. However, it was not until the fourth century that they were officially considered the New Testament Bible. The books that make up the New Testament were decided upon by three important criteria: first, their divine qualities; second, their reception by the churches; and third, their connection to an apostle. Most of the New Testament books were composed directly by one of the apostles, and those that were not had very close ties to the apostles.

One way that we determine which books were part of the Old Testament canon is to see how the New Testament writers quoted them. There is not a single instance anywhere of a New Testament author quoting a book as Scripture that is not in our current 39-book canon. And while Jesus Himself had many disagreements with the Jewish leadership of his day, there appears to be no indication that there was any disagreement over which books were Scripture—a reality that is hard to explain if the Old Testament canon was still not decided. The New Testament had solidified 22 of the 27 New Testament books by the second century. God has given us ways to recognize the books that were inspired by Him, namely those that have divine qualities, corporate reception, and authoritative authors.

When the Bible speaks—God is speaking. When you hold a Bible in your hands, you are holding the written record of the very words of God that He gave to us by divine inspiration. The Bible reveals the very words, ideas, thoughts, and teachings of God. The Bible is the record of everything that God wants us to know. Can there be anything more valuable and important to us than a book that contains all of the thoughts of the God who made us and who created everything that we see around us? What an amazing and precious book.

The Bible reveals to us the law of God.

THE TEN COMMANDMENTS

1. Thou shalt have no other gods before Me.
2. Thou shalt not make unto thee any graven image.
3. Thou shalt not take the name of the Lord Thy God in vain.
4. Remember the Sabbath day to keep it holy.
5. Honor thy father and mother.
6. Thou shalt not kill.
7. Thou shalt not commit adultery.
8. Thou shalt not steal.
9. Thou shalt not lie.
10. Thou shalt not covet.

The Bible reveals to us God's purpose for creating mankind. This is The Creation Mandate of Genesis 1:26-28:

"Then God said, 'Let Us make man in Our image, according to Our likeness; let them have dominion over the fish of the sea, over the birds of the air, and over the cattle, over all the earth and over every creeping thing that creeps on the earth.' So God created man in His own image; in the image of God He created him; male and female He created them. Then God blessed them, and God said to them, 'Be fruitful and multiply; fill the earth and subdue it; have dominion over the fish of the sea, over the birds of the air, and over every living thing that moves on the earth.'"

Man was created by God and was designed to have dominion over the creation that God made by His divine fiat. Non-Christians do not accept the doctrine of creation. The unbeliever propounds the philosophy of Naturalism. Greg Bahnsen, a defender of the faith, remarks on the absurdity of this philosophy:

"When asked if something can miraculously pop into being from nothing in an instant, the non-Christian vigorously responds in the negative. Instant miracles are out of the question!

But when asked if something can come out of nothing if given several billion years, the non-Christian confidently responds in the affirmative."[2]

The Bible reveals how all men should live and treat one another, Micah 6:8, "He has shown you, O man, what is good; And what does the Lord require of you but to do justly, to love mercy, and to walk humbly with your God?"

The Bible reveals to us how we can have eternal life through faith in Jesus Christ:

"For God so loved the world that He gave His only begotten Son, that whoever believes in Him should not perish but have everlasting life." John 3:16

"That if you confess with your mouth the Lord Jesus and believe in your heart that God has raised Him from the dead, you will be saved." Romans 10:9

The unique nature of the Bible is revealed by the following essay:

The Bible

The Bible reveals the mind of God, the need of man, the way of salvation, the doom of sinners, and the happiness of believers. Its doctrines are holy, its precepts are binding, its histories are true, and its decisions are immutable.

Read the Bible to be wise, believe the Bible to be safe, and practice the Bible to be holy. The Bible contains light to direct you, food to support you, and comfort to cheer you.

The Bible is the traveler's map, the pilgrim's staff, the pilot's compass, the soldier's sword, and the Christian's charter. In the Bible, Paradise is restored, Heaven is opened, and the gates of hell are closed. Christ is its grand subject, our God the designer, and the glory of God its end.

The Bible should fill the memory, rule the heart, and guide the feet. Read the Bible slowly, frequently, and prayerfully. It is a mine of wealth, a paradise of glory, and a river of pleasure.

The Bible is given to you in life, will be opened in judgment, and remembered forever. The Bible involves the highest responsibility, will reward the greatest labor, and will condemn all who trifle with its sacred contents. My dear friend, treasure the Word of the living God.[3]

The Bible is God's instruction book and operating manual for our daily living. This precious book provides answers for the following concerns that every man, no matter where he is born, will have.

What is...

- The origin of life?
- The meaning of life?
- The purpose of life?
- The basis of right and wrong?
- The mysteries of the universe?
- The destiny of people after death?
- The definition of truth?
- The nature of man?
- The plan of salvation?
- The meaning of the life and death of Jesus Christ?
- The way to heaven?
- The way to escape hell?
- The will of God for my life?
- The future of the human race?
- The true definition of marriage and the family?
- The purpose of the government?
- The purpose of the church?
- The purpose of the law of God?
- The plan of God for His church?

The Bible forms the basis of the only view of the world that makes any sense. The Bible gives us the absolute authority for all right and wrong and all moral convictions. The Bible serves as the basis for all logical reasoning. The Bible is the source of all truth.

- The Bible claims to be the Word of God.
- The Bible claims that God exists.
- The Bible claims that God created the world in six days.
- The Bible claims that Jesus Christ is the Son of God.

The Bible is not only the best-selling book of all time, it is year-in and year-out the best selling book every single year. Every year in the United States over 25 million Bibles are bought and distributed across the country. It is popular because it is, in fact, the Word of the living God. Furthermore, the Bible gives us the greatest story ever told. The greatest story ever told is the story of Jesus Christ the Son of God. This great story has captured the imaginations of millions of people and has given the world the most profound moral teachings in the history of mankind. The story of Jesus, as found in the Bible, is unsurpassed for the beauty, glory, and wonders of its themes. It is a story that towers over history and has filled the hearts of those who worship Jesus Christ with unceasing devotion and undying love. It has inspired the greatest religion on earth, Christianity. This great story is filled with breathtaking scenes of everlasting love, eternal sacrifice, and divine wisdom. The story of Jesus is a fountain flowing with the abundance of grace, mercy, and peace from the Creator of the world. This amazing story is found in the greatest book ever written, the Bible. The Bible is a divine drama. In the Bible we have the dramatic and breathtaking unfolding of the greatest story ever told. It is a classic story that has a beginning with creation. It contains the tragedy of the temptation and fall of man in the Garden of Eden. This great story has countless participants who play a wide variety of roles: prophets, priests, kings, sages, rabbis, villains, heroes, both good and evil, all encompass the pages in the Holy Bible. This story spans over 1500 years from the call of Abraham to the crucifixion and resurrection of Jesus Christ. For the past 2000 years since Jesus was raised from the dead, this story still lives. It is a story that pits light against darkness, good against evil, the fallen powers of darkness against the angels of light. This wonderful story is found only in the pages of the Bible, God's Holy Word.

2
Why Is The Bible True?

W e have stated that the Bible claims to be the Word of the living God. As a matter of fact, the Bible was the first book in history to make such a claim. This is a bold claim to make. We are saying when we teach this that the Bible is the very Word of God. We are saying that the words found in the pages of the Bible are the words that God has written Himself and are the exact words He wanted all of us to hear and know. Many years after the Bible was written and complete there were two other books that came along in history that also made this unique claim. The two books were the Quran and the Book of Mormon. The Bible anticipated that there would be other books that would claim to be the Word of God. The Bible warns us about such writings and tells us that if any other book made such a claim it was to be rejected. The book of Revelation chapter 22 verse18 says:

> "For I testify to everyone who hears the words of the prophecy of this book: If anyone adds to these things, God will add to him the plagues that are written in this book; and if anyone takes away from the words of the book of this prophecy, God shall take away his part from the Book of Life, from the holy city, and from the things which are written in this book."

The Bible is complete and the Quran and the Book of Mormon are cheap imitations of the Word of God and are not to be believed or accepted as the true Word of God. There are a number of reasons why we believe that the Bible is the Word of the living God.

- The Bible claims to be the Word of God.
- The Bible is self-attesting.
- The Bible was accepted by Jesus Christ as the Word of God.
- The Bible has been miraculously preserved through the centuries and has been without any major textual errors or contradictions.

The Bible Claims To Be
The Word Of God

If the Bible did not claim to be the Word of God, we would not have any reason to draw such a conclusion. It is only because the Bible claims to be God's Word that we have a reason to accept it as such and defend it from its enemies. The Bible was the first book in the history of the world that claimed to be the divinely inspired Word of God. Since then, two other books have also made a similar claim. The two books I'm thinking of are the Quran and the Book of Mormon, but these two books do not contain any internal or external evidence to verify the truth claims that they have made.

The Bible gives us a complete and truthful worldview. A worldview is a series of presuppositions that shapes and determines everything a person believes and does. According to Dr. Greg Bahnsen, a Christian apologist, a worldview relates to three main areas: Metaphysics—how we view reality, Epistemology—how we know what we know, and Ethics—conduct and morality.

A worldview answers a number of philosophical questions such as:

- Where did we come from? (creation, origins)
- Why are we here? (purpose for life)
- Why is there evil and suffering in the world? (the fall of man)
- Is there anything that we can do about evil and suffering? (salvation)
- Is there a God?
- Has that God communicated with us?
- Is there life after death?

The Bible also gives us all the information that we need for life. It gives us:

- A detailed account of our origins and creation
- A detailed list of laws and moral absolutes
- A detailed account of the first man and woman
- A detailed explanation of the Creator
  - His names
  - His attributes
  - His laws
  - His works
  - His ways

When people ask me why I believe in God, why I believe Jesus is the Son of God, or why I believe there is a God, I reply "Because the Bible says so." This is the place to start. When confronting the philosophers on Mars Hill, we see that the Apostle Paul made his appeal to the Scriptures. Acts 17:16-25 records the conversation Paul had with those unbelievers:

> "Now while Paul waited for them at Athens, his spirit was provoked within him when he saw that the city was given over to idols. Therefore he reasoned in the synagogue with the Jews and with the Gentile worshipers, and in the marketplace daily with those who happened to be there. Then certain Epicurean and Stoic philosophers encountered him. And some said, "What does this babbler want to say?" Others said, "He seems to be a proclaimer of foreign gods," because he preached to them Jesus and the resurrection. And they took him and brought him to the Areopagus, saying, "May we know what this new doctrine is of which you speak? For you are bringing some strange things to our ears. Therefore we want to know what these things mean." For all the Athenians and the foreigners who were there spent their time in nothing else but either to tell or to hear some new thing. Then Paul stood in the midst of the Areopagus and said, "Men of

Athens, I perceive that in all things you are very religious; for as I was passing through and considering the objects of your worship, I even found an altar with this inscription: TO THE UNKNOWN GOD. Therefore, the One whom you worship without knowing, Him I proclaim to you: God, who made the world and everything in it, since He is Lord of heaven and earth, does not dwell in temples made with hands. Nor is He worshiped with men's hands, as though He needed anything, since He gives to all life, breath, and all things. And He has made from one blood every nation of men to dwell on all the face of the earth, and has determined their preappointed times and the boundaries of their dwellings, so that they should seek the Lord, in the hope that they might grope for Him and find Him, though He is not far from each one of us; for in Him we live and move and have our being..."

Paul challenged his listeners with the God of the Bible. Paul's method of evangelism began with the certainty of his conviction that all men in their heart of hearts know God. Paul, when writing to the church in Rome, said the following:

"For the wrath of God is revealed from heaven against all ungodliness and unrighteousness of men, who suppress the truth in unrighteousness, because what may be known of God is manifest in them, for God has shown it to them. For since the creation of the world His invisible attributes are clearly seen, being understood by the things that are made, even His eternal power and Godhead, so that they are without excuse, because, although they knew God, they did not glorify Him as God, nor were thankful, but became futile in their thoughts, and their foolish hearts were darkened." Romans 1:18-21

Notice that Paul says, "...although they knew God, they did not glorify him as God...."

So the one who defends the faith must follow the example of Jesus, Abraham, and the Apostle Paul when sharing and defending the faith. These men began with Scripture. They did not merely present mountains of evidence and hope that their listeners would be convinced of the truth of the gospel.

The Bible Is Self-Attesting

Another reason I believe the Bible is true is because it is self-attesting. What do we mean when we say that the Bible is self-attesting? This means the Bible is its own authority and it proves itself. No other religious book from any other religion can do this. The Bible was the first book to claim to be the inspired Word of the living God. Since then, two other books have also made a similar claim. The two books are the Quran and the Book of Mormon, but these two books do not contain any internal or external evidence to verify the truth claims that they have made.

Because the Bible is self-attesting it has internal evidence that verifies its truth claims. There is no evidence outside of the Bible that can be appealed to that is greater than the Bible itself. By appealing to evidence outside of the Bible, we are putting the Bible on trial and are giving men the right to judge both God and the Bible itself. We must never assume that by stringing together a list of evidential anecdotes that we can convince unbelievers that the Bible is probably true. The Bible is true because it is the ultimate and absolute truth. It is God Himself who speaks to us from the Bible.

The Bible carries its own authority. It needs nothing outside of itself to prove its divine origin. I often defend the Bible by pointing out five things that verify its truth claims:

- Prophetically—There are hundreds of prophecies in the Bible that have been fulfilled and therefore serve as powerful evidence that the Bible is true.
- Historically—Nothing in history or archeology has ever been discovered that has cast even a shadow of a doubt on the Word of God.
- Scientifically—The Bible is not a science book but where it speaks to scientific issues it is always accurate and correct. In 1974, an article in *Time Magazine* entitled, How True Is The Bible, admitted, "After more than two centuries of facing the heaviest scientific guns that could be brought to bear, the Bible has survived—and is perhaps the better for the siege."[1]
- Morally—The Bible presents to mankind the highest and most relevant and sophisticated system of morality and ethics.
- Dynamically—The Bible when presented to mankind has its own inner witness and power to radically change the lives of those who put their trust in the gospel message that the Bible proclaims.

Jesus Christ Accepted The Bible And Taught Men That It Was True

One of the most powerful reasons that we know the Bible is true is because Jesus told us it was. Jesus gives the Bible His full backing and support. Jesus, as we know, is the eternal Son of God. We know that Jesus is the Son of God because of these five convincing reasons:

- Jesus was holy and without sin.
- Jesus fulfilled all of the Messianic prophecies from the Old Testament.
- Jesus performed many miracles.
- Jesus taught with such authority and with such amazing insights giving the world the greatest moral teachings the world has ever received.
- Jesus was resurrected from the dead, proving He was God. Dr. Greg Bahnsen reminds us, "After His resurrection Christ charged the apostles 'to preach unto the people and to testify that this is He who is ordained of God to be the Judge of the living and the dead' (Acts 10:42). Paul declared this truth in his Areopagus apologetic, going on to indicate that God had given "assurance"' or proof of the fact that Christ would be mankind's final Judge. This proof was provided by the resurrection

of Jesus Christ from the dead." Jesus is not only God come in the flesh, He is the One who will judge us in the last day."[2]

Since Jesus is God and since He gave the Bible His stamp of approval, we can be sure the Bible is true and is to be accepted as the Word of the living God.

The Bible Has Been Miraculously Preserved

We know the Bible is true and accurate because it has been preserved miraculously over the years. Textual criticism is the science of studying and comparing the text of any written ancient document to determine if the document has been preserved and is without errors of human additions and subtractions. Textual criticism is a very reliable way of ascertaining the integrity of any ancient document. How does this work? We simply ascertain how many copies we have of the original document. We categorize them by year and place where they were found or written. By studying and comparing these documents from different periods of history and from different locations, we can determine if the document is accurate and that it has been preserved through the centuries without any significant errors. The Bible, when studied by textual experts, has been shown to be without any significant errors and is considered to be one of the most authentic and reliable documents we have in our possession from the ancient world. No one who understands this discipline of textual criticism would even begin to doubt the accuracy and integrity of the Holy Bible. Frederick Kenyon, an expert on the Biblical text, concluded, "The Christian can take the whole Bible in his hand and say without fear or hesitation that he holds in it the true Word of God, handed down without essential loss from generation to generation through the centuries."[3]

3

Why Is The Bible Important?

t should be evident to anyone who studies the Bible that to have in our hands the written words, letters, instructions, warnings, and encouragements from the God of creation should be an awesome and unfathomable gift from God. To press upon people the importance of the Bible, just take them outside and have them gaze into the heavens or look at the stars at night. Then tell them, "The Creator, the God who made all things, gave us this Bible to read, study, and to be a guide and book of instruction for us on this amazing planet that He has made."

Another reason the Bible is so important to us is that it gives to each of us the answers to the most important questions in life:

- Who am I?
- Where did I come from?
- What is my purpose in life?
- Where am I going?
- Is there a God?
- Is there life after death?
- Is there a heaven and a hell?
- Who is Jesus Christ?
- What is good and what is evil?

The Bible also provides us with the absolute authority for all our moral beliefs and convictions. The following list of topics found in the Bible are absolutely necessary for us to learn and study:

- The Ten Commandments
- The ethical teachings of Jesus
- The Old Testament law
- The moral teachings found all throughout the Bible

The Bible is the only way we know the following behaviors are wrong.

- Slavery
- Genocide
- Euthanasia
- Abortion
- Discrimination
- Violence
- Unjust warfare

The Bible also teaches us that the following sources cannot provide us with an absolute authority for our faith and beliefs:

- Human governments
- Political leaders
- Cultural habits
- Earthly traditions
- Popular opinions
- Pundits and media heroes
- The majority opinions or the whims of the day
- The vote and opinion of the 51%

Without God and the Bible we cannot account for the laws of logic, the laws of reason, the existence of good and evil, the moral basis for right and wrong. How would we come to know any of these things if we did not have the written revelation of God found in the Bible? Christian philosopher Cornelious Van Til has wisely said that we need God to refute God. Without the Bible we cannot account for man's self awareness, his ultimate value, and the sacredness of his life.

Perhaps most importantly, the Bible is important because it teaches us about the gospel of Jesus Christ. The God of creation, who made all things, created the world and put man in it. Our first parents, Adam and Eve, sinned in the Garden of Eden. This is referred to as the fall of man. Because of that first act of disobedience by Adam and Eve, every child that's born since that time has a sin nature that is prone to breaking the laws of God. In order for God to allow any of us into heaven, He had to provide a way of salvation for us. This way of salvation is through the finished work of Jesus Christ. God the Father gave His only Son, the Lord Jesus, to be a sacrifice for our sins. Jesus was born of the Virgin Mary, and He lived a sinless life for 33 years. At the end of His life, Jesus was betrayed by one of His disciples named Judas. Jesus was then tried by the Jewish religious leaders and then turned over to the Roman authorities. Jesus was found guilty and was scourged by the

Roman soldiers and then they crucified Him on a cross. Jesus was buried on a Friday, but on Sunday morning Jesus Christ was raised from the dead, proving that He was the Son of God. Jesus had to live our life and die our death. This means that He lived for 33 years and never sinned. Jesus kept the laws He made Himself and rendered back to the law a perfect obedience. It is the holiness and obedience of Christ that enables us to stand in the presence of God. When a sinner puts his or her faith in Jesus, their sins are transferred to Him and are forgiven, and the holiness of Jesus is transferred to the believer, and thus, they are covered by His holiness. But it's not enough just to have the holiness of Christ covering us. Because God is holy and just, He must punish sin. And so God the Father gave His Son to be a sacrifice for us by dying on the cross for our sins. When Jesus was on the cross, all the sins of those who will eventually believe in Him were transferred to Him. And when a person believes on Christ, not only are their sins transferred to Jesus, but the holiness and righteousness of Jesus is transferred to the believer. This is called justification by faith. People are not saved by their good works but by the finished work of Jesus Christ. This is the gospel. The gospel means good news. God the Father found a way to save sinners. He takes our sin and lays it on His Son Jesus Christ. And He takes the holiness of Jesus Christ and lays it on us. So the way that we get to heaven is by repenting of our sin, which means to turn and forsake it. Then we put our faith in Christ, believing that He is the Son of God, that He lived a holy life for us, that he died on the cross for our sins, and that he rose again from the dead on the third day. No one can get to heaven unless they believe in the good news of the gospel of Jesus Christ.

Finally, let me say one last thing. Without the Bible and the precious knowledge that it imparts, we are left in a meaningless universe without any purpose or hope for our existence. How empty and lonely would life be without the knowledge of the Bible in the precious truths that it teaches us. How tragic it is that there are so many people who go through all of their life never knowing the joy in the wonder of the knowledge of God.

Let me summarize the seven reasons why the Bible is so important to every believer and child of God.

First, the Bible is the written revelation of everything God wants us to know.

Second, the Bible gives us the answers to all the philosophical and important questions in life.

Third, the Bible serves as the basis and foundation for all our moral beliefs and convictions.

Fourth, the Bible is the only way to know what God considers right and wrong.

Fifth, the Bible teaches us that there is no other authority outside of the Bible itself for our faith and beliefs.

Sixth, the Bible reveals God's plan of salvation through the gospel of Jesus Christ.

Seventh, the Bible provides the basis for a life full of meaning and purpose. For without the Bible life is empty, meaningless, and without hope.

Conclusion

There are many wonderful things about the Christian life that so many of our youth today do not understand. Let me start by saying there are things about the Christian faith that cannot be compared to anything else in the world. For example, there is no greater love than the love of God for sinners. There is no greater gift than God's gift of His Son to die for our sins. There is no greater joy than the joy of being a child of God. There is no greater privilege than to be one of the chosen. There is no greater purpose in life than to live for Christ. There is no greater message than the message of redeeming love. There is no greater peace than the peace of God. Finally, there is no greater earthly possession than to have a copy of the Word of God as your own personal love letter from the Creator Himself. How many of our young people can even comprehend what I am saying?

We have established that the Bible is the foundation of our faith and practice. Everything that we believe and how we should live our lives is spelled out for us and given to us in the Bible. If we lose the Bible we lose our culture, our history, our purpose for living, and our hope for eternal life. If God and the Bible are rejected, then anything is possible and the potential for evil is limitless. To demonstrate the authority of the Bible we have looked at three things:

- What Is The Bible?
- Why Is The Bible True?
- Why Is The Bible Important?

I remind every person who reads this book that to believe in the Bible and to read it and heed it is one of the most important decisions you can make. It is also true that to reject the Bible and the God of Scripture is by far the worst decision one can make this side of eternity. May we all treasure the Word of God. May we live by its gracious truths. May we be guided by its timeless principles. And may its wisdom, light, and inspiration motivate each of us in our daily walk and lead us, in the end, to eternal life through Jesus Christ our Lord. I close this book by leaving with each of you some precious thoughts about the wonderful book that has been given to us from our heavenly Father.

The great Methodist preacher John Wesley once said this about the Bible:

"…I want to know one thing, the way to heaven; how to land safe on that happy shore. God Himself has condescended to teach the way: for this very end he came from heaven. He hath written it down in a book. O give me that book! At any price, give me the book of God! I have it: Here is knowledge enough for me. Let me be *homo unius libri* ("a man of one book").[1]

And one of the greatest preachers who ever lived was Charles Haddon Spurgeon. He said these things about the Bible:

- "To me the Bible is not God, but it is God's voice, and I do not hear it without awe."

- "Oh, to have 'the word of Christ' always dwelling inside of us—in the memory, never forgotten; in the heart, always loved; in the understanding, really grasped; with all the powers and passions of the mind fully submitted to its control!"

- "Little as men think it, religion has much to do with our liberty, our happiness, and our comfort. England would not have been what it now is, if it had not been for her religion; and in that hour when she shall forsake her God, her glory shall have fallen, and 'Ichabod' shall be written upon her banners. In that day when the gospel shall be silenced, when our ministers shall cease to preach; when the Bible shall be chained; in that day—God forbid it should ever come to pass—in that day, England may write herself among the dead, for she hath fallen, since God hath forsaken her, seeing she hath cast off her allegiance to Him. Christian men, in this fight for right, ye are fighting for your nation, for your liberties, your happiness, and your peace; for unless religion, the religion of heaven be maintained, these will most certainly be destroyed."[2]

In this quote from C.H. Spurgeon we see that he sees the rejection of the Bible as an indication of the defeat of the Christian culture. If the Bible is forsaken and rejected the culture and the nation will be lost. The Bible is what gives Western Civilization its distinct character and elevates her above every other culture in the history of mankind. The battle for freedom, the battle for liberty is a battle over the Word of God.

Inside the cover of many of my personal Bibles I have written this poem that puts in poetic verse the love and wonder that I have for the Bible:

The Bible

Though the cover is worn, and pages are torn,
And places bear traces of tears,
Yet more precious than gold, is this book worn
and old,
That can shatter and scatter my fears.

When I prayerfully look, in this precious old
book,
As my eyes scan the pages I see,
Many tokens of love from the Father above,
Who is nearest and dearest to me.

This old book is my guide, tis a friend by my side,
It will lighten and brighten my way.
And each promise I find soothes and gladdens
my mind.
As I read it and heed it today.

Footnotes

Chapter One:

1. Billy Graham, Faith 101, What Is The Bible? August 28, 2006, BillyGraham.org.
2. Greg Bahnsen, quoted by Douglas Douma, Review: Pushing The Antithesis, by Greg Bahnsen, Book Reviews, June 9, 2018.
3. Anonymous, found in the Gideon Bible.

Chapter Two:

1. *Time Magazine*, How True Is The Bible? December, 30, 1974.
2. Greg Bahnsen, Always Ready: Directions For Defending The Faith, Covenant Media Press, pg. 271, Kindle Edition.
3. Frederick Kenyon, Our Bible And The Ancient Manuscripts, 1897, pg. 11.

Conclusion:

1. John Wesley, From the Preface of His Standard Sermons.
2. C. H. Spurgeon, The War On Truth, January 11, 1857.

www.ingramcontent.com/pod-product-compliance
Lightning Source LLC
Chambersburg PA
CBHW022345040426
42449CB00006B/727